Copyright & Disclaimer

MW00888414

Travel Like A Local (Map Book) By Maxwell Fox (2019)

About Maxwell Fox

With a taste for adventure, Maxwell Fox has always been passionate about one thing: traveling.

Ever since he was a little boy he was filled with a unique curiosity and an adventurous spirit that took him along to beautiful and amazing new experiences. From short trips with family to imaginary travels around the world, his wanderlust was his driving force from a young age.

He was fascinated by the endless possibilities of new lands, people and ways of life and that is exactly what he looked to discover every time he went on a new adventure.

From trying the local cuisine and exploring brand new flavors, to visiting all the important cultural and historical sights, he carefully planned each trip so he could experience each place to the fullest and discover every little corner.

What he was after was not the tourist experience but the unique immersion into a new community and a different culture.

So what he did was strive to experience each city like a true local.

Traveling gave him the opportunity to increase his knowledge and interest in history, culture, art, architecture and language. Through his experiences he sought to improve his skills and become the best version of himself.

After his many adventures and life changing experiences, he tried to find a path that would excite him just as much as traveling did.

So he thought of what travelers everywhere have in common and what thing brings all his interests together. And that's how he started his journey through the artful science of cartography.

With a formal training in cartography and a unique love for traveling and adventure, Maxwell Fox decided to make it his life's mission to help fellow travelers around the world have the most amazing experience every time they travel.

ACCOMMODATION

- Hotel
- Motel
- Hostel
- Camping

FOOD & DRINK

- Restaurant
- Fast food
- Cafe
- Ice cream
- Bar
- Pub

SHOP & SERVICE

- Supermarket
- Depertment store
- Marketplace
- Kiosk
- Greengrocer
- Alcohol
- Confectionery
- Bakery
- Tea
- Electronics
- Computer
- Mobile
- Hifi
- Clothes
- Shoes

- Jewellery
- Bag
- Beauty
- Perfumery
- Hairdresser
- Laundry
- Travel agency
- Books
- Art
- Gift
- Toys
- Florist

TRANSPORTATION

- Parking
- Taxi
- Bus stop
- Bus station
- Subway entrance
- Rental car
- Fuel
- Charging station
- Rental bicycle
- Aerodrome
- Helipad
- Ferry

ENTERTAINMENT, ARTS & CULTURE

- Cinema
- Theatre

Nightclub
Museum
Library
Artwork
Arts Center
Fountain
Viewpoint

FINANCIAL

Atm
Bank

ACTIVITY

Fitness
Swimming
Golf
Miniature golf
Playground

HEALTHCARE

Hospital
Doctor
Pharmacy
Dentist
Optician

POST

Post box
Post office

LAND USE

Highway
Primary road
Secondary road
Tertiary road
Unclassifield road
Railway
Tram railway
Ferry road
Water
Beach
Volcano
Border
Quarry
Comemercial
Nature
Park
Residential area

OTHER

Information
Toilets
Waste basket
Drinking water
Table
Bench
Elevator
Police
Fire station
Courthouse
Embassy

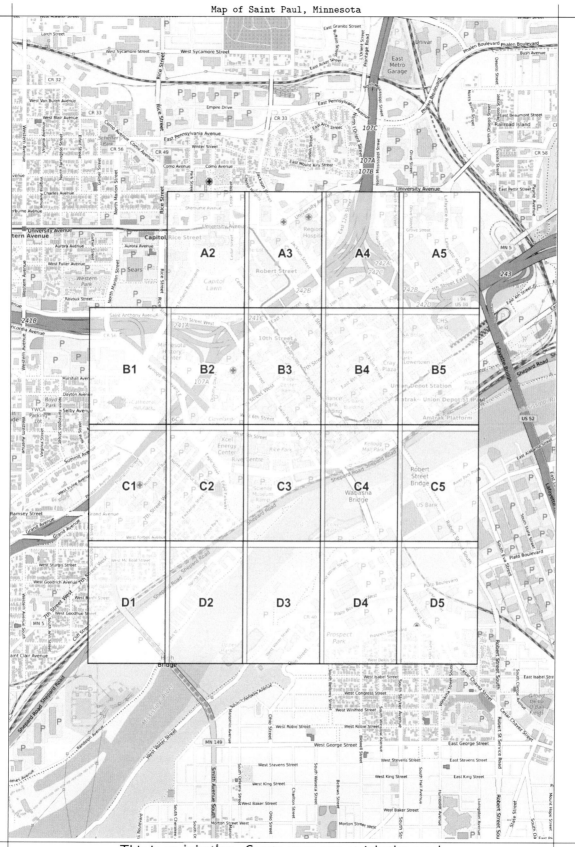

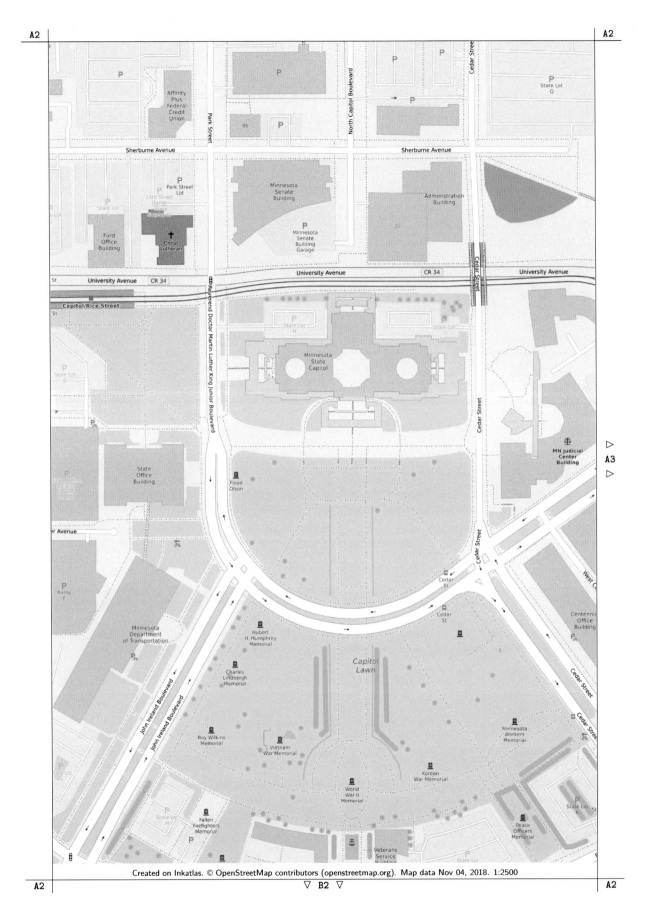

A3

Robert Street North

Jackson Street

University Avenue

Gillette Children's Specialty Healthcare

Gillette Children's Specialty Healthcare

West Patient/ Visitor Parking

Regions Hospital

P

University Av

University Avenue

14 St

14 St

Jackson Street

Regions Hospital West Lot

Emma Norton Residence

14th Street Parking Ramp

State Lot L

East 14th Street

State Lot W

State Lot U

...dicial ...ter ...ding

East Central Park Place

West Central Park Place

Orville L. Freeman State Office Building

Robert Street

Robert Street North

Harold E. Stassen State Office Building

12 St

Centennial Parking Ramp

Centennial Office Building

West Columbus Street

Freeman Lab Building

Minnesota Street

East 12th Street

Cedar Street

East 13th Street

Cedar Street Armory - Minnesota National Guard

Columbus Av

East 12th Street

East 12th Street

Robert Street North

242B

CR 34

East 11th Street

East 11th Street

11 St

City & County Credit Union

BP

BP Metropolitan Center for Independent Living

Downtown Alano Society of St. Paul

The Penfield

Caribou Coffee

State Lot K

State Lot K

East 12th Street

East 11th Street

East 12th Street

P

Created on Inkatlas. © OpenStreetMap contributors (openstreetmap.org). Map data Nov 04, 2018. 1:2500

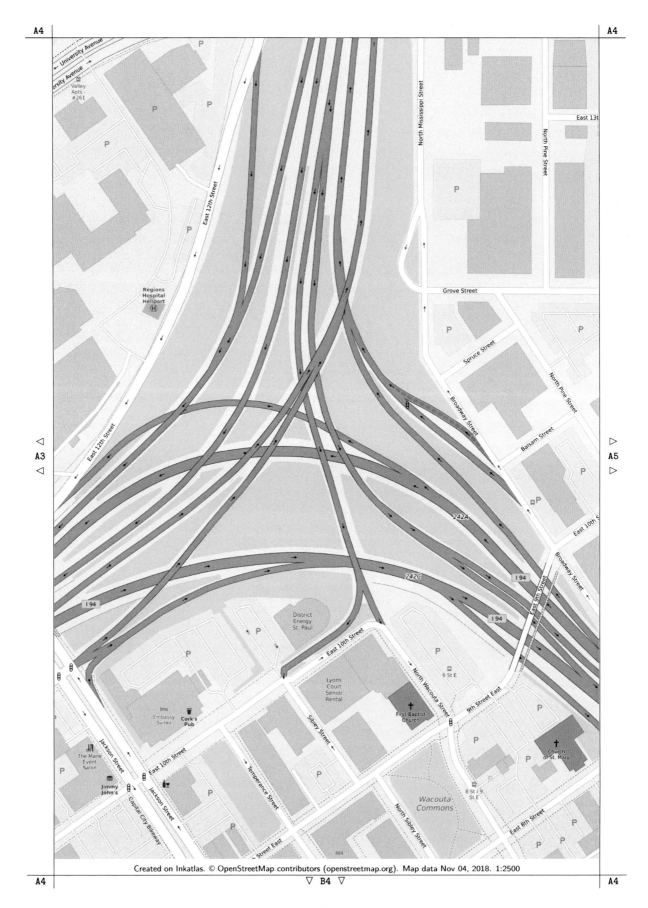

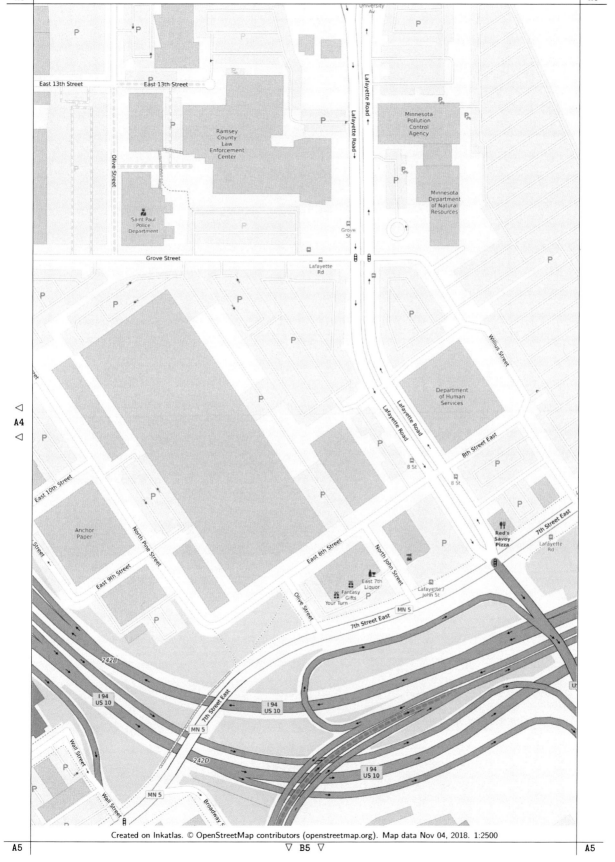

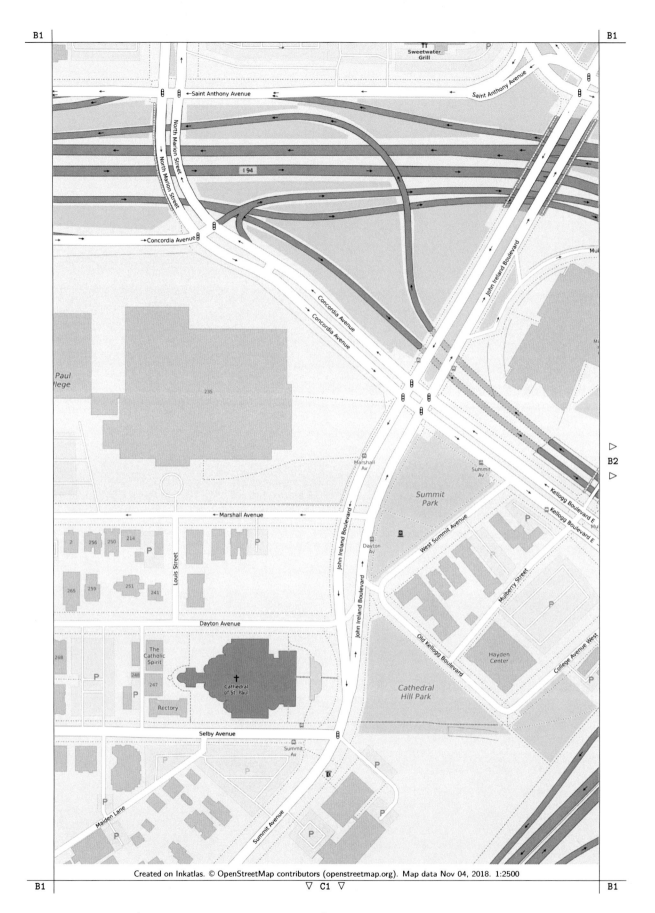

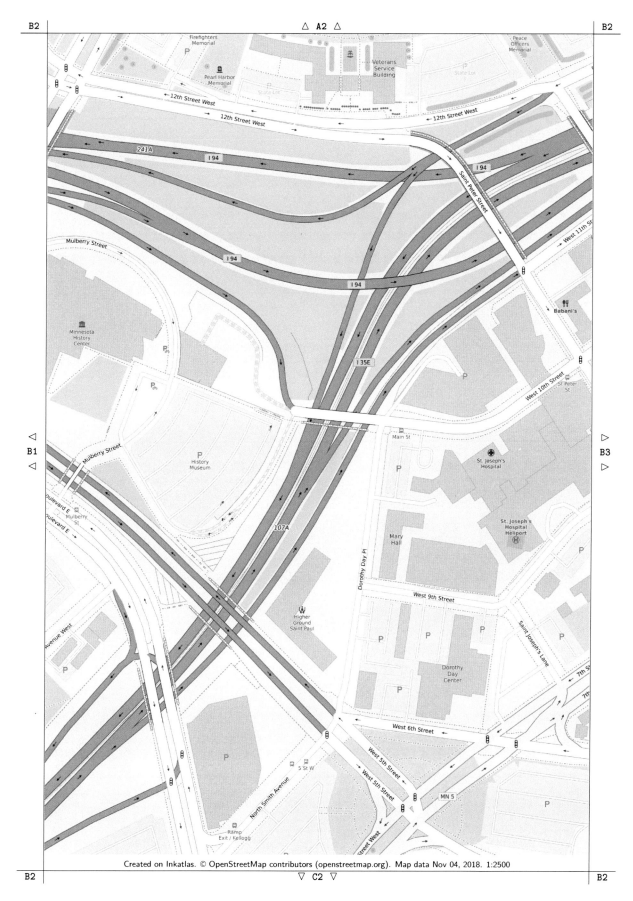

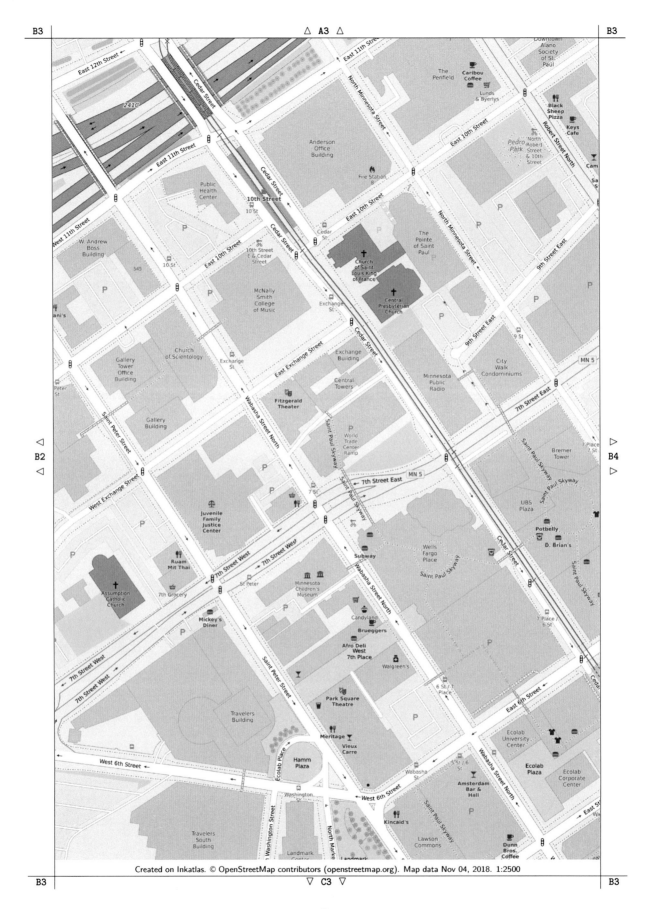

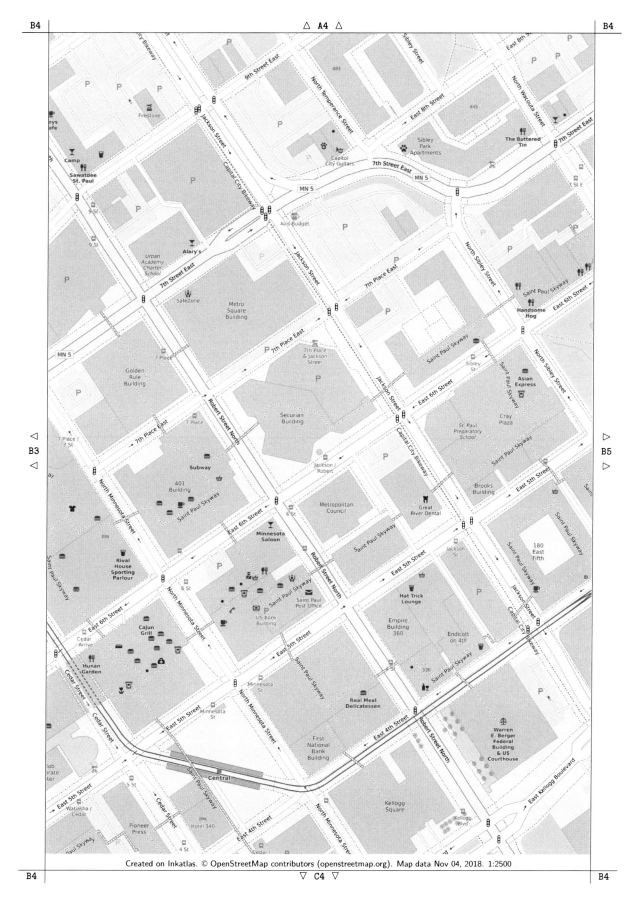

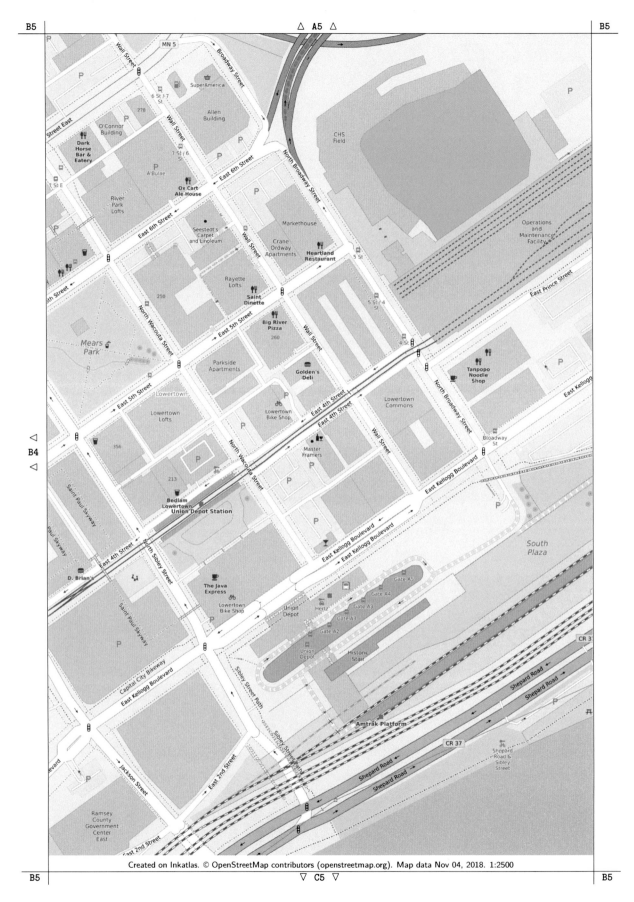

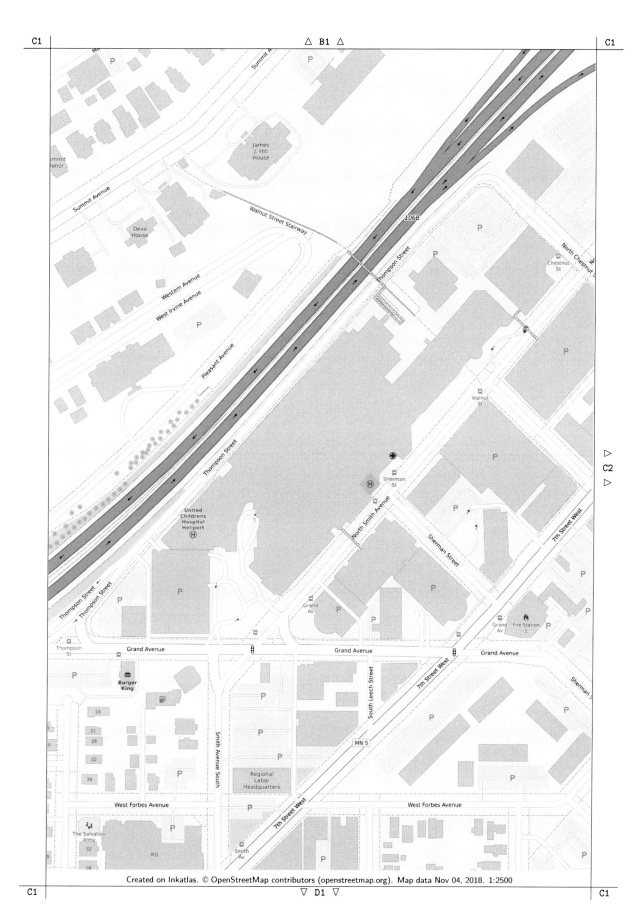

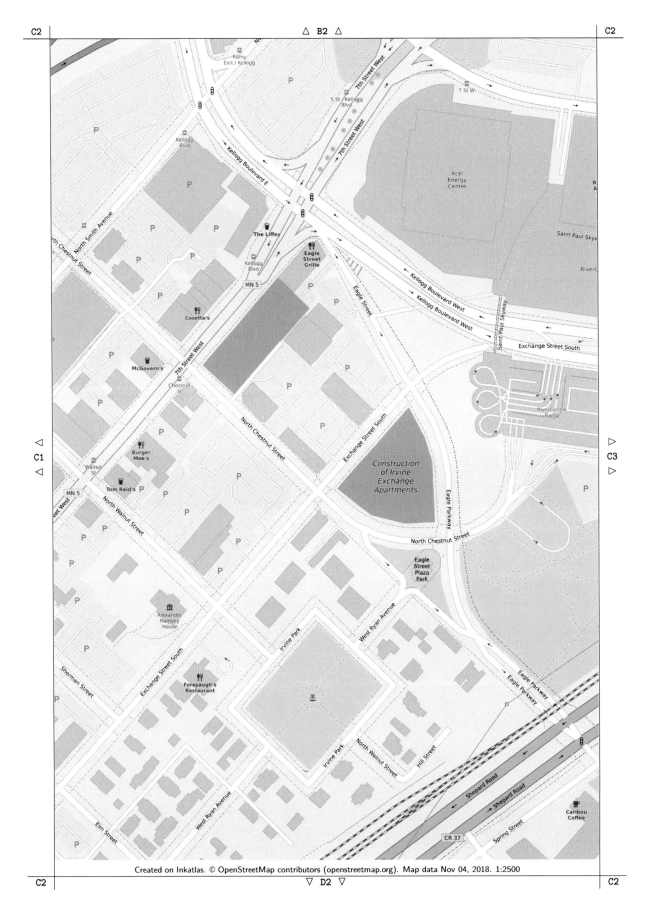

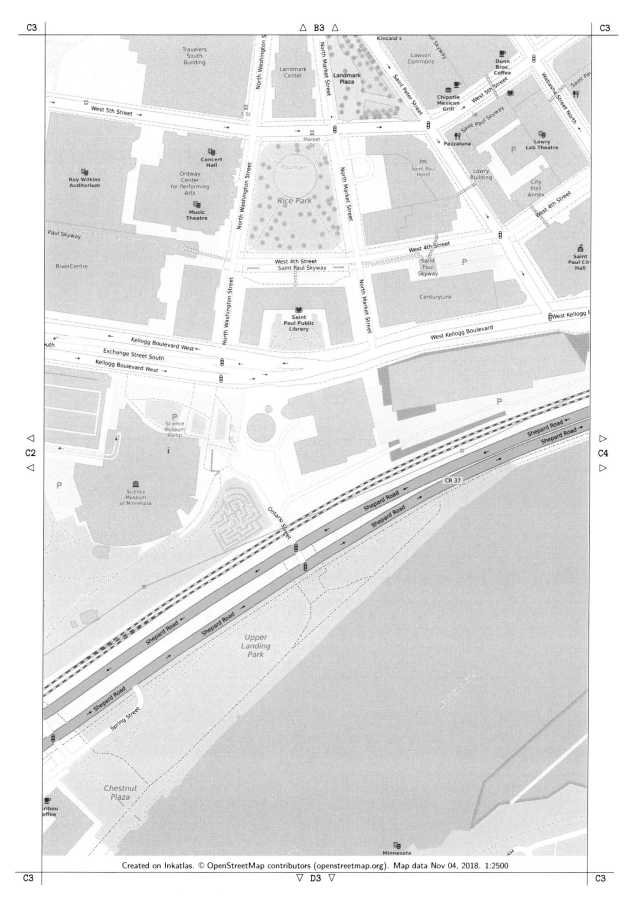

Travelers
South
Building

Landmark
Center

Landmark
Plaza

Kincaid's

Lawson
Commons

Dunn
Bros.
Coffee

West 5th Street

Concert
Hall

Ordway
Center
for Performing
Arts

Roy Wilkins
Auditorium

Music
Theatre

Chipotle
Mexican
Grill

West 5th Street

Pazzaluna

Saint Paul Skyway

Lowry
Lab Theatre

Saint Paul
Hotel

Lowry
Building

City
Hall
Annex

Market
St

Fountain

Rice Park

West 4th Street

Paul Skyway

RiverCentre

West 4th Street
Saint Paul Skyway

Saint
Paul
Skyway

P

CenturyLink

West 4th Street

Saint
Paul City
Hall

Saint
Paul Public
Library

West Kellogg B

Kellogg Boulevard West

West Kellogg Boulevard

Exchange Street South

Kellogg Boulevard West

P

Shepard Road
Shepard Road

P
Science
Museum
Ramp

P

CR 37

Science
Museum
of Minnesota

Shepard Road

Ontario Street

Shepard Road
Shepard Road

Upper
Landing
Park

Mississippi River

Shepard Road

Shepard Road

Shepard Road

Spring Street

Chestnut
Plaza

ribou
offee

Minnesota

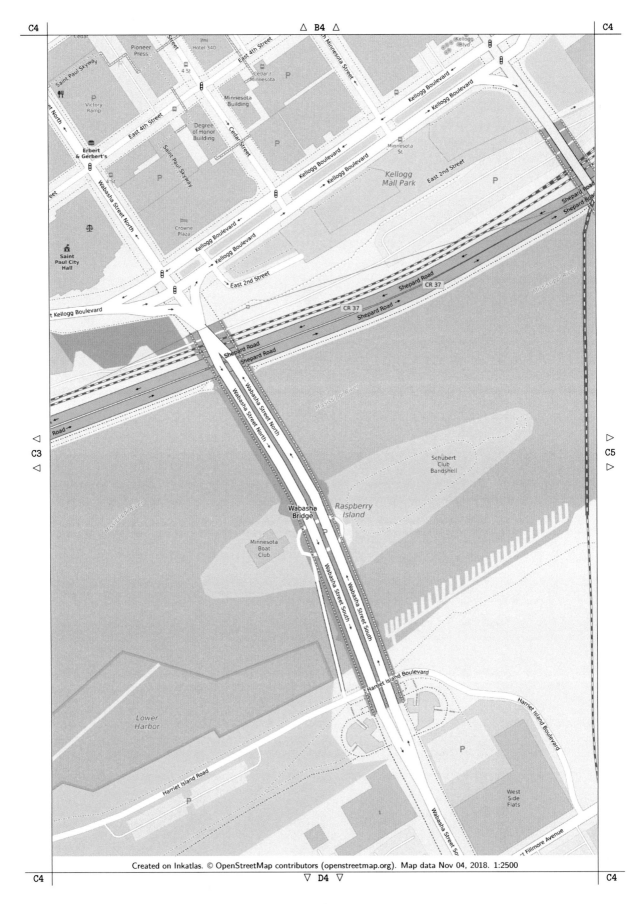

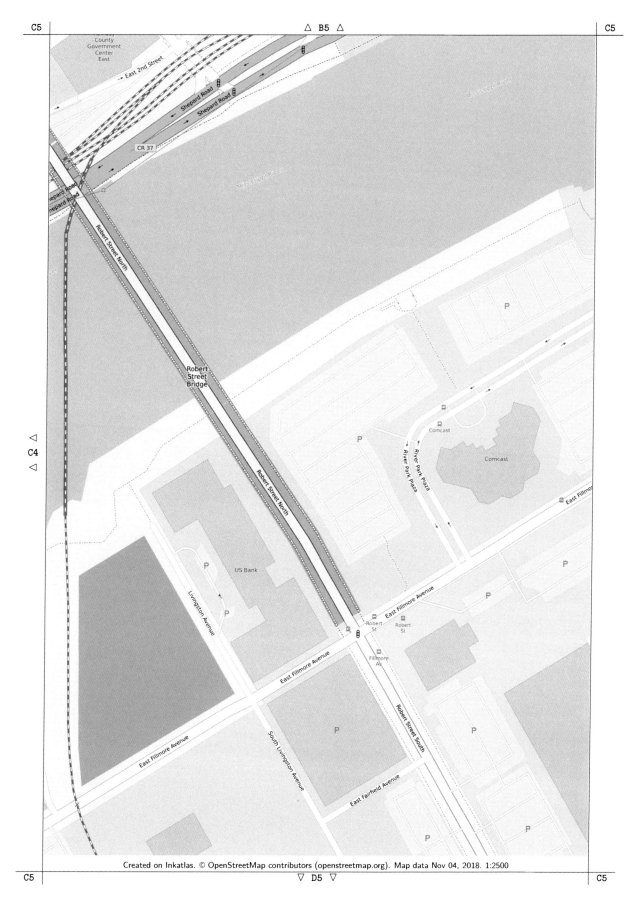

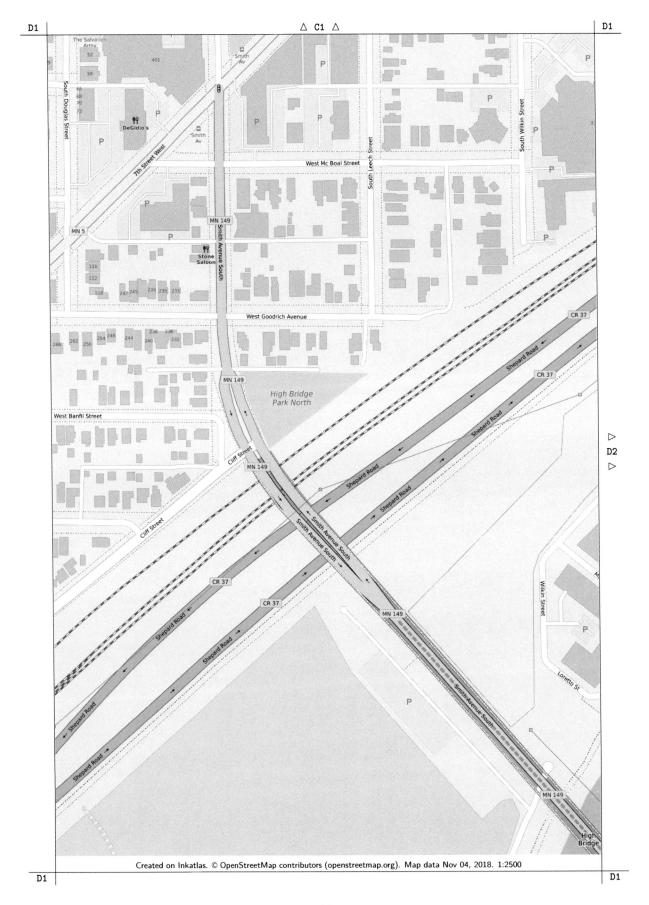

D1   D1

Created on Inkatlas. © OpenStreetMap contributors (openstreetmap.org). Map data Nov 04, 2018. 1:2500

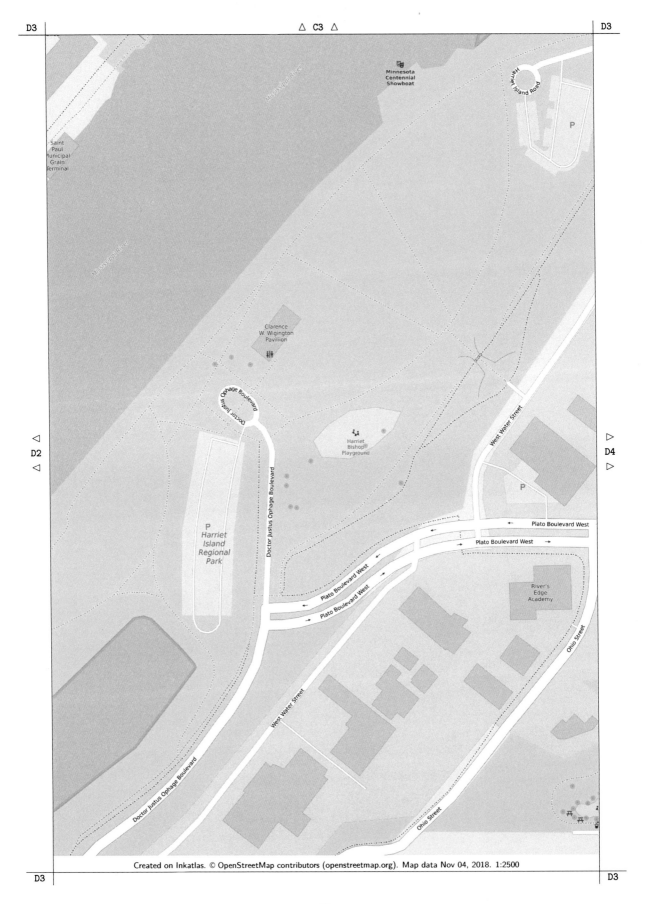

Created on Inkatlas. © OpenStreetMap contributors (openstreetmap.org). Map data Nov 04, 2018. 1:2500

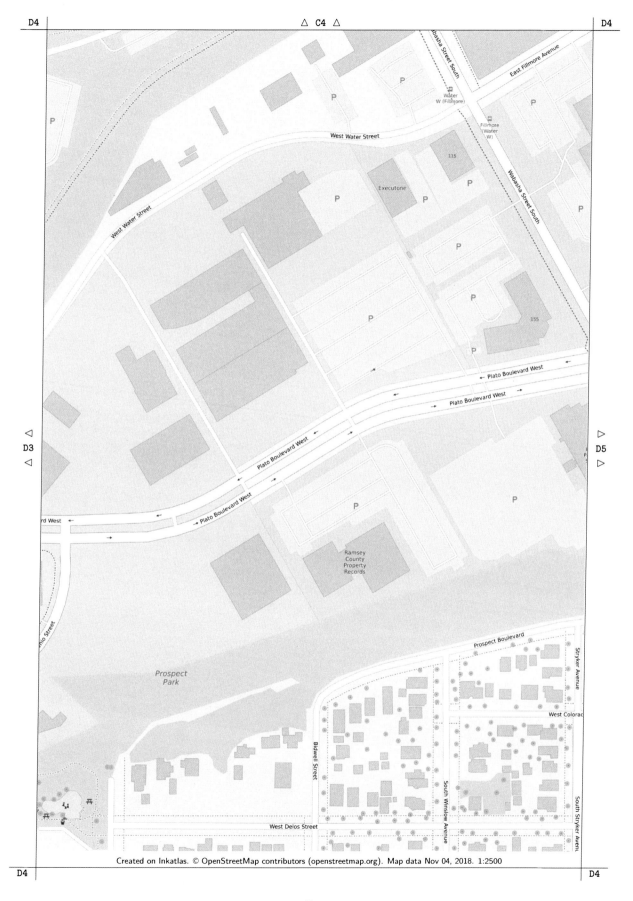

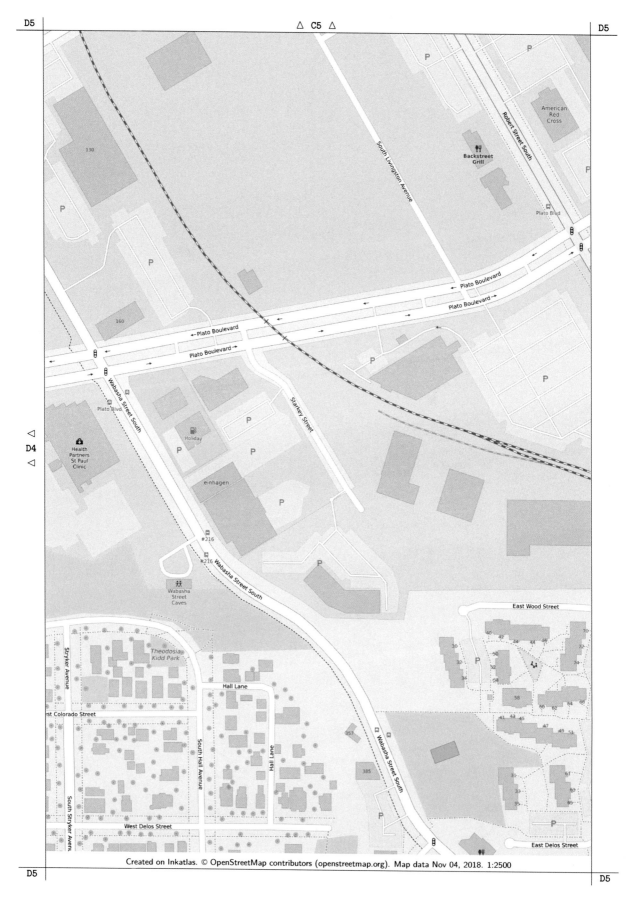

Created on Inkatlas. © OpenStreetMap contributors (openstreetmap.org). Map data Nov 04, 2018. 1:2500

Travel Planner

WHERE?

_____

_____

_____

WHEN?

FROM: ____ / ____ / ____

TO: ____ / ____ / ____

DAYS: _____

TRANSPORTATION

☐ ✈ ☐ 🚌 ☐ 🚗 ☐ ⛴ ☐ 🚲 ☐ 🚶 ☐ _____

DETAILS:

_____

_____

_____

_____

_____

_____

_____

_____

_____

_____

_____

_____

_____

Made in the USA
Monee, IL
16 July 2022

99824771R00031